# Webstein's Dictionary

by

Joel M. Stein

For
Adele,
Lily,
Shroeder,
and
Tennyson

# alta kockerspaniel

*pr.* **awl** • tuh • kahk • er • **span** • yel

n. **your grandma's 17-year old dog that shakes, urinates, and bites your ankle every time your cell phone rings**

*from the root **alta kocker**: old fart*

# bemah-meyup

*pr.* **bee** • mah • **mee** • uhp

n. **a term, particularly popular in Star Trek circles, used to denote an honorary visit to the ark during the high holidays**

*from the root* **bemah**: *raised platform in temple*

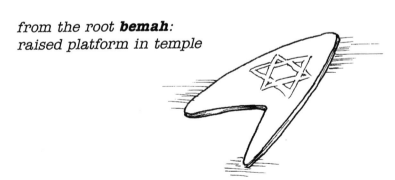

# besherbet

*pr.* beh • **sher** • bit

adj.  **the feeling you have when ordering the last scoop of blue raspberry just before the 8-year old next to you with the same intentions can beat you to it**

*from the root **beshert**: fate; meant to be*

# bissel blower

*pr.* **bi** • sel • bloh • er

n. **a woman who tells the world of your lackluster performance in bed**

*from the root **bissel**: a little*

# brisketbeef

*pr.* **bris** • ket • beef

n. **the argument you have with your butcher about whether he had his thumb on the scale or not**

*from the root **brisket**: a particular cut of meat, often prepared as a traditional Jewish dish*

# brisseling

*pr.* **bris** • el • eeng

v. **the agitated, gut-felt, sweaty-palmed state of all men (Jewish or otherwise) before, during and after this joyous rite of passage**

*from the root **bris**: ceremonial circumcision of male babies on the eighth day after birth*

# bubbelatte

*pr.* buhb • bee • **lah** • tey

n. **the morning beverage your grandma sends you to get with an expired coupon that has been on her refrigerator since your Bar Mitzvah**

*from the root **bubbe**: grandmother*

# bupkiss

*pr.* **buhp** • kis

v. **the action at the end of the night of you leaning in, lips parted, and her quick turn of her cheek to meet them, on the first and last date with someone way too hot for you**

*from the root* **bupkis**: *nothing, zilch*

# chalerious

*pr.* chah • **air** • ee • us

adj. **describing professionally-honed nastiness, as in your sister greeting you with a "good morning" that intends more to express "go screw yourself"**

*from the root **chaleria**: bitch*

# challahscopy

*pr.* khah • **lah** • skoh • pee

n.  **the procedure to remove thirty years of Friday evening white bread impacted in your colon**

*from the root **challah**: traditional braided bread served on Sabbath, and most holidays*

Webstein's Dictionary

# chazzerye

*pr.* khah • zer • **ahy**

n. **the loaf of bread your shnorer uncle devours while polishing off the last of your Kayo**

*from the root **chazzer**: pig; swine-like*

# chutzpawed

*pr.* **khootz • pawd**

v. **the action of your aunt's dog jumping on your new white pants, followed by, "Honey, it's after Labor Day anyway..." from your aunt**

*from the root* **chutzpah***: unmitigated gall*

# drek tech

*pr.* **drek** • tek

n. **the shleppy guy in the IT office whose sole purpose is to ruin your computer every time he runs a Windows update**

*from the root **drek**: crap*

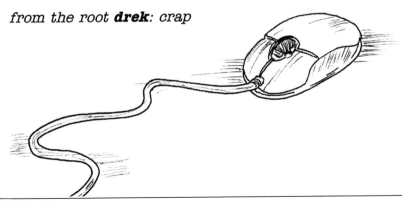

# drunk davening

*pr.* druhnk • **dah** • ven • eeng

## v. the rocking motion as you pray for the room to stop spinning after a big night of Purim

*from the root **daven**: rhythmic rocking motion used in prayer*

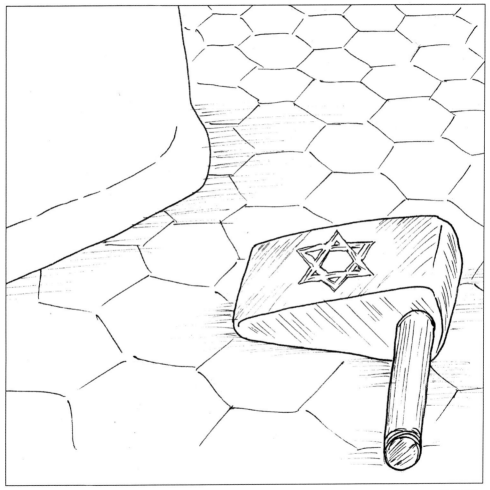

# farcocktail

*pr.* fahr • **kokt** • eyl

n. **the expensive drink sent to the woman across the bar not realizing her muscular husband was returning from the bathroom**

*from the root **farcockt:** all screwed up*

# fast-talker

*pr.* **fast** • taw • ker

n. **the person at shul who must
tell you how they have not eaten
anything, drunk anything, or even
brushed their teeth, the evidence
of which wafts in your face
throughout Neilah**

*from the root **fast**:
to not eat, or drink,
relating to Yom Kippur*

# fermishion

*pr.* fer • **mish** • uhn

n. **a fleeting state of confidence experienced between waves of sheer anxiety about whether your garage door actually closed as you arrive at the Goldberg's for dinner**

*from the root **fermished**: confused*

# furklempt

*pr.*  fer • **klemp** • t

adj.  **the feeling you get when your husband finally presents to you a ranch-raised, black-diamond mink coat (all-female skins, of course)**

*from the root **farklempt**: all choked up over something*

# geshmak-down

*pr.* ge • **shmak** • down

n. **the long-standing kugel feud
between your two grandmas,
requiring you to seat them at
opposite ends of the table**

*from the root* **geshmak**: *tasty*

# goyimpulse

*pr.* goy • **im** • puhls

n. **the sudden urge to forsake your family by marrying the cute Catholic barrista at Starbucks**

*from the root* **goyim***: non-Jewish folks*

Webstein's Dictionary

# hondl bars

*pr.* **hahn** • duhl • bahrs

n. **nightclubs open until 4 a.m. catering to last-call romance**

*from the root **hondl**: to bargain*

# jewkbox

*pr.* **jook** • box

n. **the iPod containing tracks from Neil Diamond's "Jazz Singer," the entire "Sex In The City" soundtrack, and every Beastie Boys album — all seven of them**

*from the root **jew**: person of the Jewish faith*

# kishkeynote speaker

*pr.* **kish** • kee • noht • **spee** • ker

n. **the position into which you are thrust when the person you hired to give a speech for your shul's huge black tie benefit is a no-show**

*from the root* **kishke**: *guts; also a meatless sausage dish served in the intestinal casing of cow*

# knishues

*pr.* k • **nish** • oos

n. **the problems that develop in your intestines following the ingestion of one of your grandma's unrecognizable "delicacies"**

*from the root **knish**: a baked pastry containing any one of a number of fillings (potatoes, kashi, etc.)*

# koorvaette

*pr.* **kohr** • vuh • **et**

n. **the little red sports car in which the suspicious neighbor woman ferries men around**

*from the root **koorva**: slut*

# krephlachdown

*pr.* **krehp** • lahk • down

n. **the state you find yourself in when your grandmother will not leave the kitchen until you have eaten enough for seven light battallions**

*from the root **kreplach**: ravioli filled with meat, onion, and chicken fat, served in soup*

# kvell ling

*pr.* k • **vel** • eeng

n. **the old woman at the dry cleaners who can never say enough wonderful things about your husband**

*from the root **kvell**: to burst with pride, usually of a loved one*

# kvetchtables

*pr.* k • **vech** • tuh • buhls

n. **the couple in the restaurant who sends each course back to the kitchen with specific instructions on how to properly prepare their food**

*from the root **kvetch**: to complain*

# l'chai-ham

*pr.* li • **khahy** • ham

n. **the last bone-in HoneyBaked™ on the after-Easter clearance rack for which you also have a double coupon**

*from the root **l'chaiem**: a celebratory cheer or toast meaning "To Life!"*

# macherana

*pr.*  mah • kher • **ey** • nah

n.  **the dance performed by your brother-in-law every time he talks about his stock portfolio**

*from the root **macher**: big shot (in the pejorative sense)*

# mishpuchell

*pr.* meesh •puh • **khel**

n. **your entire family of seventeen... oh, and your sister's dog, her friend, Tammy (and her dog), your uncle's girlfriend, and the woman your uncle used to date whom everyone keeps forgetting to take off of last year's invite-list**

*from the root **mishpuchah**: the whole family*

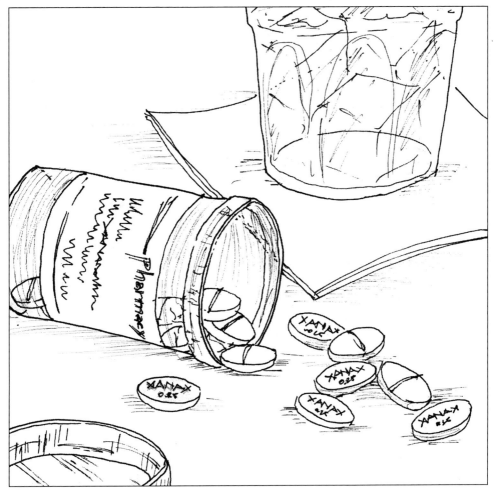

# mishuganauts

*pr.* mi • **shoo** • gah • nawts

n. **the courageous pilots willing to ride into space aboard thirteen thousand tons of metal constructed by the  low-bidder**

*from the root **mishuggah***: *crazy*

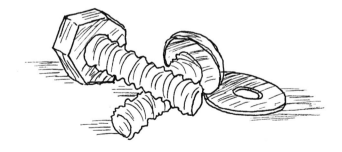

# north shnorer

*pr.* nohrth • **shnohr** • er

n. **the individual who comes near the end of every holiday meal — when they have been elsewhere — to eat, drink, and leave with sacks of leftovers**

*from the root **shnorer**: a mooch*

# nudjitsu

*pr.* nooj • **it** • soo

n. **the combative art of annoying the hell out of you so-practiced by your family that they should offer classes**

*from the root **nudje**: to pester*

# ongepatchkate

*pr.* uhn • ge • **pahch** • keyt

adj.  **describing the way your sister wore her hair, and her bathing suits, circa 1988-89.**

*from the root **ongepatchket**: overly decorated, or too busy, in terms of style*

# Passoverture

*pr.* pass • **oh** • ver • cher

n.  **the annual declaration that everyone else is able to make it home for both meals — even those from out of town. "And you!  You live forty minutes away.  You can't come home to celebrate two nights out of the year?"**

*from the root **Passover**: the religious holiday celebrating the Jewish exodus out of Egypt*

# pesadickies

*pr.* **pey** • sah • dik • ees

n. **the same pair of pants your father has worn for the last seventeen passover dinners because the charroset-stain on the right thigh bares a striking resemblance (in his mind) to Moses**

*from the root **pesadicky**: Passover-specific kosher*

# pilpullover

*pr.*  pil • **pohwl** • oh • ver

n.  **a simple conversation with your wife that ends with you stopping the car and re-evaluating every life choice you have made up to that point**

*from the root **pilpul**: a discussion that loses its main thrust, and devolves into hair-splitting minutia*

# pupickle

*pr.* puh • **pik** • el

n.  **an inability to wear a bikini in front of your parents because you and Tammy had your belly-buttons pierced last spring at Club Med**

*from the root **pupik**: belly button*

# Purim bastard

*pr.* **poor** • im • bas • terd

## n. **a child conceived out of wedlock on a crazy, drunken holiday**

*from the root **Purim**: religious holiday celebrated in carnival-style on the 14th day of Adar*

# reubenesque

*pr.* roo • ben • **esk**

adj. **the shape you assume after routinely gorging on sandwiches swimming for their lives in Thousand Island dressing**

*from the root* **reuben***: deli sandwich consisting of corned beef, sauerkraut, and thousand island dressing on rye bread*

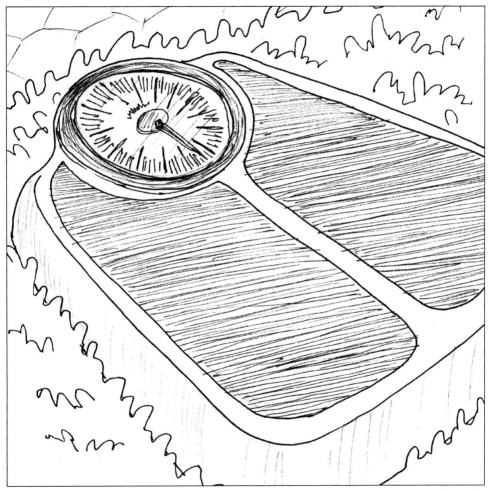

# Rosh Hashananigans

*pr.* **rohw** • sh • hah • shah • nan • i • gens

n. **the chaotic annual ritual your family practices in which each member questions, then debates, the others over which night of the holiday everyone is eating at the Goldberg's**

*from the root **Rosh Hashanah**: the Jewish New Year holiday traditionally celebrated on two consecutive days and nights*

# ruggallaw

*pr.* **roo** • guh • law

n. **the statute that a quantity of pastries brought to a dinner party must twice-exceed the number of attendees (unless your grandma is attending, in which case, nothing you bring will be good enough because she did not make it, so don't bother)**

*from the root **ruggallah**: flakey butter dough dessert filled with preserves, or chocolate*

# sadorachmonesism

*pr.* sey • doh • rok • **mown** • es • ism

n. **the act of your mother telling you that you look "a little thick" in your new dress, then handing you her credit card to go buy something "more flattering"**

*from the root* **rachmones**: *pity; sympathy*

# salamiopic

*pr.* sah • lahm • ee • **op** • ik

adj. **the inability to focus on anything your wife says because of the piled-high deli sandwich in front of you**

*from the root **salami**: cured air-dried sausage meat that is a staple of Jewish delis*

# shallowm

*pr.* sha • **lowm**

n. **the insincere greeting you receive from your neighbor who cannot stand you, but lusts for your wife, according to your other neighbor**

*from the root **shalom**: greeting of peace*

# shikkerah

*pr.* shi • **keer** • uh

n. **the uncle that drinks heavily at the holidays, resulting in an awkward "My Hips Don't Lie" routine**

*from the root **shikker**: a drunk*

# shiksicle

*pr.* **shik** • sih • kuhl

n. **that tasty treat-of-a-woman who serves you your latte as you meander through the drive-thru on your way to High Holiday services**

*from the root **shiksa**: a non-Jewish woman*

# shmaltz-liquor

*pr.* sh • mawltz • **lik** • er

n. **rum and diet soda garnished with two lemon wedges, a lime, three blue cheese olives on the side, and another phone number from the not-so-recently divorced**

*from the root **shmaltz**: over the top; over-done*

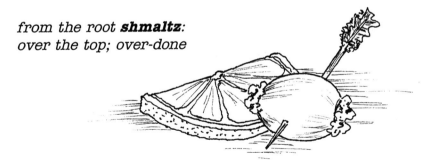

# shmattempt

*pr.* shmah • **temp** • t

v. **the action of trying to leave the house in jeans, a t-shirt, and flip-flops en route to your in-laws' barbeque**

*from the root **shmatta**: a rag*

# shmeckelectomy

*pr.* shmek • el • **ek** • to • mee

n. **a declaration made by your wife in front of your friends that your attendance at the annual golf trip would be occasional, at best**

*from the root **shmeckel**: penis*

# shmendrix

*pr.* **shmen** • driks

n. **the doofus next to you on the plane with the huge headphones, mouthing the words to his music**

*from the root* **shmendrik**: *a loser; dork*

# shmoozic

*pr.* sh • **mooz** • ik

n. **the conversation you have with the person next to you in line while waiting to get a "Best of Barry Manilow" autographed CD for your boss' mother-in-law**

*from the root **shmooze**: to chat*

# shtickball

*pr.* sh • **tic** • bawl

n. **a game played between two smart-asses to see who can out-quip whom, despite being part of a minyan**

*from the root* **shtick**: *an act or routine*

# shtupendous

*pr.* shtuhp • **pen** • duhs

adj. **describing the sex you have with your wife after you tell her you shorted the market before the Dow plunged**

*from the root **shtup**: literally to push, but used colloquially to describe the act of sex.*

# shul-operative

*pr.* shuhl • **op** • er • uh • tiv

n. **the heavy guy at the temple door on high-holidays wearing all the acoutrements of a Secret Service agent, and sweating**

*from the root* **shul**: *temple*

# toochismoney

*pr.* **tookh** • his • muhn • ee

n. **a large divorce settlement painfully extracted from you by the young shiksa (for whom you left your first wife of thirty years), and her attorney boyfriend**

*from the root **toochis**: butt*

# treyf bien

*pr.* **treyf** • bee • awn

n. **a ham purchased on sale around Easter time, but disguised as a corned beef to hide it from your aging mother-in-law**

*from the root* **treyf**: *un-kosher*

# treyfywife

*pr.* **treyf** • ee • wahyf

n. **the 27-year old shiksa who claims to your friends, and your ex-wife, that you are the hottest 64-year old man she has ever met**

*from the root* **treyf***:*
*un-kosher*

# tsimisstaken

*pr.* **tsi** • mi • stey • khun

v. **assuming the dish your mother-in-law made looked and smelled like she would be serving it to her shi tsu, only to find it on your plate at dinner time**

*from the root **tsimmis**: meat stew with carrots and prunes*

# tsorism

*pr.*  **tsohr** • iz • m

n.  **the industry of mothers who travel to the furthest reaches of personal grief and heartache in search of whose child has married the least successful man**

*from the root **tsoris**: troubles; emotional pain*

# tunklectomy

*pr.*  tuhn • kohl • **ek** • too • mee

n.  **the procedure you give your father, by way of lecture, intended to keep him from making any racist jokes under his breath to you about some of the guests coming for dinner**

*from the root **tunkle**: literally "dark," but used in the pejorative-sense*

# varffetch

*pr.* vahrf • **fech**

n. **the international pastime of Hasidic dogs, played with ball or stick**

*from the root **varf**: to throw*

# whora

*pr.* **hohr** • uh

n. **the uncomfortably-close dance your divorced cousin performs at every wedding with every man — single or otherwise.**

*from the root **hora**: traditional Jewish circle dance*

# yenteam

*pr.* **yen** • teem

n. **two or more individuals committed
to spreading news as though it were
an international competition**

*from the root* **yente**: *to gossip*

# yiddlock

*pr.* **yid** • lok

n. **the state you find yourself in after twelve years of marriage to a woman whose father is also your business partner**

*from the root **yiddlach**: the Jews*

# Acknowledgements

The first and grandest thank you belongs to my wife. Thank you, Adele, for allowing this book to happen. Were it not for your encouragement, I would likely have shelved the whole idea like so many others before it. Honestly, it took a shiksa to make sure that the Jewish guy can realize a dream. I love you, Adele.

A special thank you to Linda Cassady of Milkweed Studio is necessary. Linda's collaborative spirit, and perfectionism (smacking of OCD,) genuinely influenced the direction of this book. Additionally, Linda's execution of the illustrations was better than all of the ideas I had for them in the first place.

Finally, thank you to Brad, Michael, and Aaron for your willingness (over beers) to help glean the good from the bad, and thank you to Julie Winsberg for additional design support and sincere enthusiasm for the whole project.